The Happy Prince

STARTER LEVEL   250 HEADWORDS

OXFORD
UNIVERSITY PRESS

Great Clarendon Street, Oxford OX2 6DP

Oxford University Press is a department of the University of Oxford.
It furthers the University's objective of excellence in research, scholarship,
and education by publishing worldwide in

Oxford New York

Auckland Cape Town Dar es Salaam Hong Kong Karachi
Kuala Lumpur Madrid Melbourne Mexico City Nairobi
New Delhi Shanghai Taipei Toronto

With offices in

Argentina Austria Brazil Chile Czech Republic France Greece
Guatemala Hungary Italy Japan Poland Portugal Singapore
South Korea Switzerland Thailand Turkey Ukraine Vietnam

OXFORD and OXFORD ENGLISH are registered trade marks of
Oxford University Press in the UK and in certain other countries

This edition © Oxford University Press 2010

The moral rights of the author have been asserted

Database right Oxford University Press (maker)

First published in Dominoes 2008

2019

25 24 23

ISBN: 978 0 19 424712 2 BOOK
ISBN: 978 0 19 463929 3 BOOK AND AUDIO PACK

No unauthorized photocopying

Printed in China

This book is printed on paper from certified and well-managed sources.

ACKNOWLEDGEMENTS

Illustrations by: Andrea Wicklund/Sari Levy Creative Management Ltd

The publisher would like to thank the following for permission to reproduce photographs: Alamy
Images pp24 (Victorian slum/Mary Evans Picture Library), 40 (Peter Pan statue/Robert Estall
photo agency), 40 (Hachiko statue, Shibuya, Tokyo/Christian Kober), 40 (Pocahontas statue/
Ange), 41 (Don Quijote & Sancho Panza/Robert Harding Picture Library Ltd), 41 (Oscar
Wilde statue/Lebrecht Music and Arts Photo Library), 42 (Woman swimming wearing
mermaid costume/Chris A Crumley); Bridgeman Art Library Ltd pp0 (An Angel Playing
a Flageolet (w/c), Burne-Jones, Sir Edward (1833-98)/Private Collection), 0 (The Prince
Regent, later George IV (1762-1830) in his Garter Robes, 1816 (oil on canvas), Lawrence,
Sir Thomas (1769-1830) / Vatican Museums and Galleries, Vatican City, Italy /Giraudon);
Corbis p0 (swallow /Roger Tidman) p41 (Statue of Mollah Nasreddin/Reza/Webistan); Getty
Images pp0 (Lord Mayor of London/Tim Graham), 42 (Man dressed as Aladdin/Michael
Goldman); iStockphoto p42 (Woman dressed as Rapunzel); Mary Evans Picture Library p24
(Barefoot match-girl); Photolibrary pp0 (Michelangelo's David/William Floyd Holdman/
Index Stock Imagery); Press Association Images pp42 (Boy dressed as Pinocchio/Joel Andrews/
AP); Rex Features p41 (The Little Mermaid statue/Richard Sowersby) p0 (Bullrushes /Lynne
Carpenter), 42 (snow queen /Kuz'min Pavel).

DOMINOES

Series Editors: Bill Bowler and Sue Parminter

The Happy Prince

Oscar Wilde

Text adaptation by Bill Bowler

Illustrated by Andrea Wicklund

Oscar Wilde was born in Dublin, Ireland in 1854, and studied Greek and Latin at university in Dublin and Oxford. As well as a number of short stories for adults and fairy stories for children, he wrote the novel *The Picture of Dorian Gray* (1891). He also wrote a number of very popular comedies for the theatre, including *The Importance of Being Earnest* (1895), but is perhaps most famous for his many clever and funny sayings about life and people. He died in Paris in 1900 at the age of forty-six. *Lord Arthur Savile's Crime and Other Stories* by Oscar Wilde is also available as a Domino.

OXFORD
UNIVERSITY PRESS

BEFORE READING

1 Match the words with the pictures. Use a dictionary to help you.

- [ ] prince
- [ ] statue
- [ ] swallow
- [ ] reed
- [ ] mayor
- [ ] angel

2 *The Happy Prince* is a fairy tale. What do you think happens? Make sentences with the things from Activity 1.

    a The . . . is in love with the . . . .

    b The . . . is always happy.

    c The . . . cries a lot.

    d The . . . wants to go to Egypt.

    e The . . . doesn't like the old . . . .

    f The . . . dies in the end.

    g The . . . comes down from the sky to find something.

3 Compare your ideas with a partner.

Chapter 1 ❈ Happy and In Love

In a country far away, a young **prince** lives happily in the wonderful **palace** of **Sans-Souci**. Nothing **sad** comes through the door of that palace. Every day he plays with his friends in the palace garden. Every night he laughs and sings with his friends in the biggest room in the palace. Everything there is beautiful. But what about the **other** people in his country? The prince doesn't know about them. He never leaves the palace or its garden. So he never thinks about other people, and he never asks any questions to learn about them. Everyone at the palace calls him, 'The Happy Prince.' And when he dies, they make a **statue** of him.

prince the most important man in a little country

palace a big house where a prince lives

Sans-Souci /sɒn ˈsuːsi/

sad not happy

other different

statue a picture of a person made of metal or stone

column a tall thing with a statue or building on it

city (*plural* **cities**) a big and important town

gold an expensive yellow metal

sapphire an expensive blue stone

ruby a very expensive stone that is usually red

The statue of the Happy Prince stands on a tall **column** over the **city**. He has **gold** all over him from head to foot. His eyes are two **sapphires**, and there is a big red **ruby** in his **sword**. All the people in the town love him.

'He's very beautiful,' says one of the Town **Councillors**, 'but he can't *do* very much.'

When a little boy begins crying for something new to play with, his mother says to him:

'Why can't you be happy? The Happy Prince never thinks of crying for new things.'

2

A sad, tired man looks up at the wonderful gold statue. He says quietly, 'Well, there's one truly happy man in the city. That's something!'

Some poor young students walk past in their red coats. They see the sun on the prince's sapphire eyes and they say, 'Look! He's an **angel**!'

Their teacher hears this, and quickly says to them, 'What are you talking about? What do you know about angels?'

'We see them in our **dreams**,' say the children.

'Well stop dreaming then,' says their teacher angrily.

sword a long, sharp knife for fighting

councillor an important man that looks after a town

angel a very good and beautiful person; in pictures they often have wings

dream pictures that you see in your head when you are sleeping; to see pictures in your head when you are sleeping

bird an animal that can fly through the sky

swallow a bird that lives in the north in the hot months and goes south in the cold months of the year

reed a tall thin plant that lives near or in water

river water that moves through the country in a long line

fly to move through the air

round on all sides of, in a circle

Earlier that year, in the country far from the city, a little **bird**, a **swallow**, meets a **reed** by the **river**. The reed is tall and beautiful and the swallow likes her at once.

'Shall I love you?' he asks her openly. She says nothing, but moves her head slowly up and down. The swallow **flies round** and round her happily.

The other swallows laugh at him and his love, the reed.

'She has no money, and she comes from a very big family,' they say. It's true. Lots of other reeds live with her near the river. But the swallow doesn't listen to his friends. He likes his summer love story.

When the **summer** finishes, the other swallows fly away to Egypt. They leave the swallow with his love. After six weeks with only the reed to talk to, he isn't very excited by her any more.

'She says nothing to me. Does she love me?'

The reed moves beautifully in front of him.

'She loves her home, but I like visiting different countries. So she must come with me.'

In the end, he asks her, 'Come away with me!'

But the reed moves her beautiful head left and right. She doesn't want to leave her nice home by the river.

So the swallow says sadly, 'All right. Then I'm going to Egypt without you. Goodbye!' and he flies away.

summer the hot time of the year

READING CHECK

Match the characters from Chapter 1 with the sentences.

a The prince never thinks about other people when he lives in his palace.

b .... is now a beautiful gold statue.

c All the people in the city love ....

d .... loves someone tall and beautiful.

e .... lives near the river.

f .... doesn't want to leave home.

g .... wants to go to Egypt.

WORD WORK

1 Find words from Chapter 1 to match the pictures.

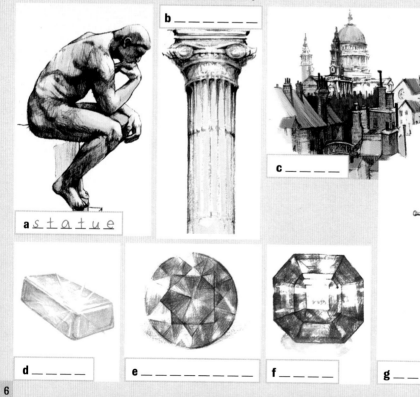

a s t a t u e

b _ _ _ _ _ _ _

c _ _ _ _ _

d _ _ _ _

e _ _ _ _ _ _ _ _ _

f _ _ _ _ _

g _ _ _ _ _ _

h _ _ _ _ _ _

i _ _ _ _ _

j _ _ _ _ _ _

k _ _ _ _ _ _ _

2 Use the words in the ruby to complete the sentences.

a Many swallows go to England in the .. summer ...

b In my .... I'm sometimes a bird and I can
....

c The young prince is never .... when he plays
with his friends.

d The swallow stays behind when the ....
swallows go to Egypt.

e Every day for six weeks the swallow flies .... the reed.

GUESS WHAT

What happens in the next chapter?
Tick two boxes to finish each sentence.

a The Happy Prince . . .

    1 ☐ begins to cry.

    2 ☐ leaves his column.

    3 ☐ talks to the swallow.

b The swallow . . .

    1 ☐ flies to Egypt.

    2 ☐ talks to the Happy Prince.

    3 ☐ feels sorry for the Happy Prince.

Chapter 2 ❦ Why is it Raining?

All through the day the swallow flies, and at night he arrives in the big city. 'Where can I stay here? Where can I find a bed to sleep in?' he thinks, and then he sees the statue of the Happy Prince on its tall column.

'I can stay here,' he says, 'From here I can look down at the town and up at the open sky, too.'

So he sits between the feet of the Happy Prince, and he looks about him. 'Tonight I have a beautiful gold room to stay in,' he says quietly, and then he begins to go to sleep.

Suddenly a big **drop** of water **falls** on him. Soon after that, a second drop hits him on the head, too.

'That's **strange**. It's raining! Reeds like the rain but not swallows.' he says. 'I must find a better bed to sleep in. This statue isn't any good in the rain. But, wait a minute. The sky's **clear**. I can't understand it.'

Just then, when the swallow is opening his wings to fly away, a third drop of water falls on him. The little bird quickly looks up. And what does he see?

He sees the sad eyes of the Happy Prince. **Tears** are running down the statue's gold face, and falling down on the swallow at his feet. The Happy Prince is crying! His face looks very sad and beautiful, and the little bird feels very sorry for him.

'Who are you?' asks the swallow.

'I'm the Happy Prince,' the statue answers.

'Then why are you crying on me?' asks the bird.

'My name comes from happier times,' says the statue, and he tells the swallow all about those past days in the Palace of Sans-Souci. 'But now I'm dead, and I'm standing

drop a small round piece of water

fall to go down suddenly

strange not usual

clear you can see it easily; nothing is in front of it

tear the water that comes from your eye when you cry

up here. I have only a **lead heart** now. But I must cry because – from here – I can see all the **poor** people and all the **ugly** things in my city.'

'So the statue isn't all gold,' thinks the swallow, but he's a bird from a good family, and so he says nothing to the prince about it.

lead very heavy grey metal

heart the centre of feeling in somebody

poor without money; something you say when you feel sorry for someone

ugly not beautiful

Then the statue says quietly.

'Far away there's a poor house in a little street. Near the open window sits a tired woman at a table. She's working, and her hands don't stop moving. She's making an evening dress for one of the young **ladies** at the palace. It has beautiful red flowers on it. In a little bed across the room from her, her son lies ill with a **fever**. He asks for

lady an important woman from a good family

fever when you get very hot because you are ill

something nice and cold to drink, but his mother can give him only river water and so he does not get well. Swallow, Swallow, please **pull** the ruby from my sword, and take it to her. My feet can never leave this column, so I cannot move from here.'

'But my friends the other swallows are waiting for me. At this time of the year they fly up and down the Nile from Cairo and talk to the Egyptian water-flowers there. I must fly away to be with them,' says the little swallow.

pull to move quickly nearer you

ACTIVITIES

READING CHECK

Choose the correct pictures.

a Where does the swallow stop in the big city?

 1 ✓

 2 ☐

 3 ☐

b What hits the swallow on the head?

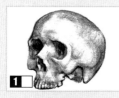 1 ☐

 2 ☐

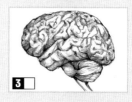 3 ☐

c What does the statue of the Happy Prince have in it?

 1 ☐

 2 ☐

 3 ☐

d What sad thing does the Happy Prince see?

 1 ☐

 2 ☐

 3 ☐

e What does the Happy Prince want to give to the woman?

1 ☐

2 ☐

3 ☐

WORD WORK

Use the words in the column to complete the sentences.

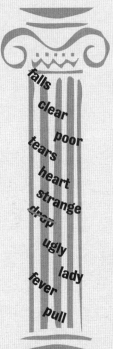

a A ......drop...... of water hits the swallow on the head.

b Usually she wears trousers but today she's wearing a skirt.
That's ....

c The swallow sees .... on the Happy Prince's face.

d The Happy Prince's .... isn't gold.

e The Happy Prince is sad because he can see ....
people.

f The little boy feels hot because he's ill with a ....

g That new building isn't beautiful. It's very ....

h She's a .... with a lot of money and she lives in a
big house.

i The Happy Prince says, '................. the ruby from my sword.

j Some water .... on the swallow's head.

k When the sky is ...., there isn't any rain.

falls
clear
poor
tears
heart
strange
drop
ugly
lady
fever
pull

GUESS WHAT

What does the swallow do in the next chapter? Tick three sentences.

a ☐ He flies away to meet the other swallows in Egypt.

b ☐ He stays in the city for a night to help the Happy Prince.

c ☐ He leaves the ruby in the river for the beautiful reed.

d ☐ He takes the ruby to the woman with the little boy.

e ☐ He helps the little boy to sleep.

f ☐ He visits lots of important people in the city.

Chapter 3 ❈ Doing Something to Help

'Swallow, little Swallow, please stay with me for only one night,' says the statue. 'You can help me. That poor boy is very thirsty and his mother is very sad.'

'I don't like boys very much,' says the swallow. 'They like hitting little birds with **stones**. I remember last summer, two bad boys down at the river . . .'

The Happy Prince looks sadly at the swallow. The little bird feels sorry for him. He doesn't like saying 'no' to people.

'. . . But I can fly fast, after all. It's very cold here now, but – yes – I can stay with you for one night and help you.'

'Thank you, little Swallow,' says the prince.

So the swallow takes the ruby from the prince's sword.

He flies away across the city with the expensive red stone in his mouth.

When he flies past the palace, he sees a beautiful young lady. She is standing at an open window and a young man is standing next to her.

'What a wonderful night!' says the young man, and he looks up at the clear sky. 'And what a wonderful young woman you are!'

'Is my new evening dress ready? I must wear it soon,' says the young woman. 'I want to see the dark red flowers all over it. Why can't these dress-makers work more quickly?'

stone something grey or white, and hard

ship you use a ship to go across the water

The little swallow flies on across the river. He flies over little old shops, and past big **ships**, to the poor house in the little street with the boy and his mother in it.

The mother is sleeping in her chair when he arrives. The boy's head is hot with fever, and he cannot sleep. The little bird flies into the room and puts the big ruby on the table near the woman's hand. Then he flies round the bed. He makes the boy's head **cool** with his **wings**.

'That's nice!' says the boy. 'I'm feeling better now.' And he stops moving about in the bed, and starts sleeping.

When the boy goes to sleep, the swallow flies back to the Happy Prince.

'It's strange,' he says, 'It's a cold night, but I feel very warm now.'

'That happens when you do something good to help someone,' says the prince.

The little swallow thinks a lot about this. Then he feels tired and he goes to sleep. He always feels tired when he thinks a lot.

The next day, early in the morning, the swallow flies down to the river for a **bath**. 'Tonight I'm going to Egypt,' he thinks happily. Through the day he flies round the town and visits all the important buildings there. An old man sees him in the sky and says, 'That's strange! A swallow here at this time of the year!' And he writes a long letter about it to the **newspaper**.

When night comes, the little swallow flies back to the Happy Prince.

'What do you want from Egypt?' he asks. 'I'm leaving now.'

'Swallow, Swallow, little Swallow,' says the prince. 'Please stay with me one night more!'

'But my friends the other swallows are waiting for me. Tomorrow they fly up the River Nile to Luxor.'

cool not warm

wing birds fly with two of these

bath when you wash all your body in water

newspaper people read about things that happen every day in this

READING CHECK

Are these sentences true or false? Tick the boxes.

		True	False
a	The swallow likes little boys a lot.	☐	☑
b	He wants to fly away because it's very cold.	☐	☐
c	He stays to help the Happy Prince.	☐	☐
d	He flies across the city with the Happy Prince's sword in his mouth.	☐	☐
e	The poor woman sees the swallow fly into the room.	☐	☐
f	The swallow leaves the ruby on the poor woman's table.	☐	☐
g	The boy feels better after the swallow flies round his bed.	☐	☐
h	The swallow feels cold when he goes back to the Happy Prince.	☐	☐
i	The Happy Prince asks the swallow to stay in the city one more night.	☐	☐

WORD WORK

Correct the sentences about the pictures with words from Chapter 3.

a There are a lot of stories *(stones)* on the road.

b It's a beautiful bird with red things.

c He's reading today's wallpaper.

d That shop is from Egypt.

e 'I'd like a nice fool drink.'

f The children are having a both in the river.

GUESS WHAT

What happens in the next chapter? Tick two boxes.

a ☐ The Happy Prince feels sorry for more poor people.

b ☐ The Happy Prince feels sorry for the swallow.

c ☐ The swallow flies to Egypt.

d ☐ The swallow pulls out one of the Happy Prince's eyes.

Chapter 4 ❀ More and More to Do

'Swallow, Swallow, far away across the city I see a poor young man. He's working at a table in a little **attic** room. He's writing a **play** for the **theatre**. He has some dead flowers next to him, his hair is brown, his mouth is red, and there are wonderful dreams in his big brown eyes. But he's very cold and hungry, and he can't think or write any more.'

'I can wait one more night,' says the swallow, because he has a good heart. 'Shall I take him a ruby, too?'

'Sadly, I have no more rubies,' says the prince. 'Now I have only the sapphires in my eyes. They come from India. Pull out one of them, and take it quickly to that poor young man. Then he can **sell** it for some good things to eat, and some warm things to wear, and – after that – he can finish his play.'

'Dear Prince, I can't do that!' cries the swallow.

'Swallow, Swallow, little Swallow, you must!' says the prince.

So the swallow takes out one of the prince's blue eyes. He flies with it in his mouth to the little attic room. The young man is tired, and he has his head in his hands on the table when the little bird arrives. He does not hear the swallow's wings. The little bird leaves the sapphire on the table near the flowers, and then flies away.

Suddenly the young man looks up and sees the expensive blue stone.

'What's this?' he cries happily. 'Someone likes my work a lot! Now I can finish my play!'

attic a little room at the top of a house

play a story that people act

theatre a building where people go to see plays

sell to take money for something

The next day the little swallow flies down to the sea. First he watches a big ship arrive from a far country. Then he sees people come from the city and take the things from it.

'I'm going to Egypt!' cries the swallow, but nobody listens to him.

When night comes, he flies back to the Happy Prince.

'I'm here to say goodbye,' he says.

'Swallow, Swallow, little Swallow, please stay with me one night more!' says the prince.

'It's cold here now, and the **snow** is coming. But in Egypt it's warm, and the sun is hot and yellow in the blue sky. My Prince, I must leave you, but I can't forget you. And when I come back next year, I can bring you a ruby and a sea-blue sapphire. I want to give you back your **missing** eye, and the expensive red stone from your sword,' says the swallow.

But the prince says quietly, 'In the town **square** under us, there's a poor little girl. She's selling **matches**. But her matches are all on the street at her feet, and she can't sell them now. Nobody wants to **buy** matches with water on them. Her father's at home. He's waiting for her. But he's always angry with her, and he hits her when she comes home with no money for him. She's crying. She has no shoes on her feet and no hat on her head. Pull out my other eye and take it to her.'

'I can wait one more night, but I can't pull out your other eye,' cries the swallow.

'Swallow, Swallow, little Swallow,' says the prince, 'you must do this for me!'

snow something soft, cold and white

missing not there

square an open place in a city with four sides

match you use this to light a fire

buy to give money for something

READING CHECK

Choose the correct words to complete these sentences.

a The Happy Prince sees a poor young singer / writer.

b He wants the swallow to take one of his eyes / hands.

c The swallow flies to the young man's room with some gold / a sapphire.

d The young man doesn't see the swallow / sapphire.

e The swallow goes to Egypt / the sea the next day.

f He wants to go to Egypt that night / the next morning.

g The Happy Prince wants the swallow to stay / go away.

h The Happy Prince talks to / sees a poor little match girl.

i When the girl goes home with no money, her father is angry / sad.

j He tells the swallow, 'Take my other eye to the girl / father.'

WORD WORK

Complete the sentences with the words in the boxes.

a The young man lives in a room in an _attic_. `c a t t i`

b He wants to _ _ _ things to eat, but he doesn't have any money. `y u b`

c 'Romeo and Juliet' is a _ _ _ _ by Shakespeare. `l a p y`

d The statue of the Happy Prince is in the town _ _ _ _ _ _. `r a u e s q`

e You can see 'Hamlet' at the Globe _ _ _ _ _ _ _ in London. `t r e e h a t`

f It's very cold and there's a lot of _ _ _ _ on the streets. `n o w s`

g The Happy Prince thinks, 'The young man can _ _ _ _ the sapphire and finish writing his play.' `e l l s`

h The little girl's _ _ _ _ _ _ _ fall down onto the street. `s t e m c h a`

i Where's my bag? I can't find it! It's _ _ _ _ _ _ _. `s i n g s i m`

GUESS WHAT

What happens in the next chapter? Tick the boxes.   Yes   No

a The swallow takes out the Happy Prince's other eye. ☐ ☐

b The swallow gives some money to the little girl. ☐ ☐

c The little girl takes the swallow to her house. ☐ ☐

d The Happy Prince can't see. ☐ ☐

e The swallow goes to Egypt. ☐ ☐

f The swallow gives gold from the Happy Prince to the poor people. ☐ ☐

g The poor people in the town are happier. ☐ ☐

h The poor people give things to eat to the swallow. ☐ ☐

Chapter 5 ❖ The Prince is Blind

In the end, the swallow pulls out the prince's other eye, and takes it in his mouth down to the town square. The little girl is standing there and crying. He flies past her and leaves the sapphire in her hand. She looks at the beautiful blue stone carefully.

'That's nice!' she cries happily, and then she runs off home with it.

Then the little bird flies back to the prince.

'You are **blind** now, and so I must stay with you always,' he says.

'No, little Swallow,' answers the poor prince, 'You must fly away to Egypt and the sun.'

'I'm staying with you now,' the swallow says. That night he sleeps at the prince's feet.

blind when you can't see

The next day the swallow sits on the prince's **shoulder**
and tells him stories of Egypt. He speaks of the river Nile,
the little towns and important cities, Egyptian people, their
work, and all the strange and wonderful things to see in
Egypt.

'My little Swallow,' says the prince. 'You tell me all these
things about Egypt, but truly I want to know more about
the people here in my city. Fly out over the town, little
Swallow, and look down. What do you see there? When
you finish, come back and tell me everything.'

shoulder this
is between your
neck and your
arm

So the little bird flies out over the big city and sees the lives of all the people there. He sees big expensive houses with poor **beggars** at their doors.

He comes back and tells the prince about hungry children with white faces in the dark streets . . .

. . . and poor cold boys with nowhere to sleep.

'Take off my **gold leaf** and give it to all the poor people. Perhaps it can make them happy.'

So, leaf by leaf, the swallow takes the gold from the statue. Now the Happy Prince looks old and grey. The little bird takes the gold leaf to the poor people. With it they can buy things to eat and things to wear. The children look better, their faces are redder and fatter, and they laugh and play in the street.

beggar a person who asks other people for money in the street

gold leaf a very thin covering of gold on something

'We have bread to eat now,' they cry happily.

Then the first snow falls, and the city streets are white with it, and very cold. The rich people wear their warmest clothes, and boys in red hats play in the snow by the river.

The poor swallow is very cold, but he loves the Prince very much and doesn't want to leave him. He finds and eats **crumbs** in front of the **baker's** shop when the baker isn't looking. And he moves his wings a lot to stay warm, but it's no good. Slowly he begins to feel colder and colder.

crumb a very little piece of bread

baker a person who makes bread

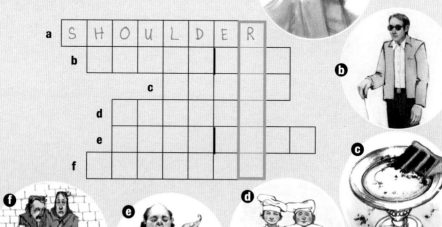

READING CHECK

Correct the sentences.

a The swallow gives the other ~~ruby~~ *sapphire* to the little girl.

b The Happy Prince tells the swallow, 'You must fly to Denmark.'

c The swallow tells the Happy Prince stories about England.

d The Happy Prince wants to hear stories about the people in the palace.

e The swallow takes stones from the statue to the poor people.

f The swallow feels very warm in the snow.

WORD WORK

1 Complete the puzzle.

a S H O U L D E R

b

c

d

e

f

2 Read the blue squares in the puzzle on page 30 to find the name of an important Egyptian king.

R _ _ _ _ _

GUESS WHAT

How does the story end? Tick one box.

The story has a . . . ending.

a ☐ sad   b ☐ happy

c ☐ sad and happy

The little swallow is dying from the cold, and he knows it. It isn't easy for him, but he flies up and sits on the prince's shoulder for the last time.

'Goodbye, my Prince,' he says quietly. 'Can I kiss your hand?'

'Ah, good. You're going to Egypt, little Swallow. I'm happy about that,' says the prince. 'It's wrong of you to wait here any more. But **kiss** me on the mouth before you go.'

'I'm not going to Egypt!' replies the swallow. 'I'm going to the house of the brother of sleep. I'm dying, you see.'

Then the little bird kisses the Happy Prince on the mouth . . .

kiss to touch lovingly with your mouth

crack a sudden noise of something breaking; a thin line that breaks something

break to go into little pieces

. . . and at once he falls down dead at the statue's feet.

Suddenly, there is a strange **crack** from the statue. The prince's lead heart **breaks** in two.

It is truly a very cold winter that year.

Early the next morning, the **Mayor** and the Town Councillors are walking in the town square. They walk past the Happy Prince's column, and the Mayor looks up at the statue on it.

'Oh dear. What an ugly grey thing our prince is these days!' he cries.

'Yes, very ugly,' say the Town Councillors. They always say everything again after the Mayor says it. All of them go nearer to the statue, and look at it carefully.

mayor the most important man in a city

law something
that tells you
what you must or
must not do

'Where's the ruby in his sword? Where are his sapphire eyes? And where's all his gold leaf?' says the Mayor. 'He doesn't look any better than a beggar.'

'No better than a beggar,' say all the Town Councillors after him.

'And look at that! There's a dead bird at the foot of his column. That's very bad. We must make a new **law**. "No birds can die in the town square."'

One of the Town Councillors writes this down in a book.

Because the statue isn't beautiful now, they take it away . . .

. . . and they **melt** it in a big **furnace**.

'Now we can make the lead from the Happy Prince into a new statue,' says the Mayor. 'A statue of me!'

'Of me! Of me!' say the Town Councillors after him, and they don't stop all talking at the same time.

melt when something hard begins to be soft or liquid

furnace this is hot, it has a door, and you melt things in it

'That's strange,' says one of the furnace workers. 'This lead heart with a crack in it doesn't melt. We must **throw** it **away**.'

So they throw the Happy Prince's heart away on the town **rubbish heap**. It falls next to the body of the little dead swallow.

Soon after that, **God** speaks to one of his angels.

'Bring me the two most important things in the city,' he says.

The angel flies down to the rubbish heap. It finds the lead heart with the crack in it, and the dead swallow there . . .

throw away to put something away because you don't want it

rubbish heap a number of things that people do not want any more, one on top of the other

God an important being who never dies and who decides what happens in the world

. . . and it brings these two things back to God.

'You're right,' says God. 'Because now this little bird can sing happily in my garden **forever** – and the Happy Prince can live in my city of gold for ever, too.'

forever always, for all time

READING CHECK

Choose the correct picture.

a The swallow says goodbye to . . . .

 **1** ☐

 **2** ☐

 **3** ☑

b The Happy Prince's . . . breaks.

 **1** ☐

 **2** ☐

 **3** ☐

c The Mayor walks in the town square with . . . .

 **1** ☐

 **2** ☐

 **3** ☐

d The Town Councillors take the statue away to a . . . .

 **1** ☐

 **2** ☐

 **3** ☐

e Someone puts the swallow on a . . . .

 **1** ☐

 **2** ☐

 **3** ☐

f The angel takes . . . to God.

 **1** ☐

 **2** ☐

 **3** ☐

WORD WORK

Write out the sentences with words from Chapter 6.

a The Councillors put the Happy Prince in a .

The Councillors put the Happy Prince in a furnace.

b Before the swallow dies he the Happy Prince.

c There's a in the Happy Prince's heart.

d The Happy Prince's heart when the swallow dies.

e The doesn't like the old statue.

f It's hot today and the snow is .

g Can I these old newspapers?

h They put the Happy Prince's heart on a .

PROJECTS

Project A *Statues with a story*

1 Read about the statues. Complete the website with the words from the box.

day film flies listening playing sitting
speaking standing story train waiting wearing

STATUES WITH A STORY

This statue of Peter Pan is in Kensington Gardens, London. In the a) _____ of Peter Pan (1911) by J.M. Barrie, Peter b) _____ down from the sky into the park and stops here. The statue of Peter is standing on an old tree and c) _____ a pipe. The fairies and little animals round the tree are d) _____ to the pipe music.

At Shibuya e) _____ station in Tokyo, Japan, there's a statue of a dog. Everyone in Japan knows about Chu-Ken Hachiko f) _____ here for his owner, Mr Ueno, every g) _____ in the 1920s. There's a Japanese film and a children's book about Hachiko's story. The statue of Hachiko is h) _____ in front of the station.

This statue of the American Indian Princess Pocahontas is in Jamestown, Virginia. There's a Disney i) _____ about her, but Pocahontas is a famous woman in the history of North America, too. The statue is j) _____, looking in front of her, and is k) _____ an Indian dress. Perhaps she's l) _____ to her father, Powhatan.

40

2 Look at the statue in the photo. Choose the best words to complete the sentences about it.

a This statue is of Oscar Wilde / Nasreddin Hodja / Don Quijote (and Sancho Panza) .

b You can see the statue in Akşehir, Turkey / Madrid, Spain / Dublin, Ireland .

c The person in the statue is from a book by Spanish writer Miguel Cervantes / a famous British writer / an old storyteller and teacher, famous for his funny stories .

d He's a thin man in armour, with a beard / fat man with a beard, with a big turban on his head / smart man in a green and pink jacket, grey trousers and black shoes .

e He's lying on a rock looking at something and smiling / sitting on a big horse / sitting on a little donkey, with a long stick in his right hand .

3 Write about the statue in Activity 2. Use the completed sentences to help you.

4 Chose another statue with a story. Make notes about it.

Name of statue:

Where is it?

Is it a real person / a character from a book or fairy tale?

Describe the statue:

5 Write about your statue. Use the website on page 40 to help you.

Project B   *Fairy Tale Roleplay*

**1 Look at these fancy dress costume pictures.
Which of these fairy tales do you know? Tell a partner.**

Rapunzel

Aladdin

The Little Mermaid

Pinocchio

The Snow Queen

2 Match these phrases with the fairy tale characters in Activity 1.

   a doesn't like being poor, wants to be rich

   b lives under the sea, wants to marry the prince

   c wants to be a real boy, his nose gets longer when he tells lies

   d has a very cold heart, lives in a big empty palace in the far north

   e has very long hair, lives in a tall tower (with no door) in the forest

3 A role card tells you who you are in a play. Read the role card for the Happy Prince. Correct seven mistakes.

Your name:	The Happy Prince
Your description:	A gold statue with ruby eyes. You're standing on a tree. You've got a newspaper in your hand.
Your habits:	You laugh a lot at things in the city.
You like:	Helping rich people.
You don't like:	Seeing angry poor people.
Your personality:	Kind. You're often happy.
Your dream:	To help people.

4 Complete the role card for the swallow.

Your name:	*Swallow*
Your description:	_____
Your habits:	*You _____ round the town all day. You _____ at the statue's feet in the evening.*
You like:	*The beautiful _____. The _____. Being in _____ countries.*
You don't like:	*Being _____. _____ – because they hit birds with _____.*
Your personality:	*You never say _____ when people ask for help.*
Your dream:	*To _____ and _____ there.*

5 Choose two fairy tale characters. Make role cards for them.
Use the role cards in Activities 3 and 4 to help you.

Your name: _____
Your description: _____
Your habits: _____
You like: _____
You don't like: _____
Your personality: _____
Your dream: _____

Your name: _____
Your description: _____
Your habits: _____
You like: _____
You don't like: _____
Your personality: _____
Your dream: _____

6 Choose a fairy tale character to be. Ask and answer questions with other students.
Guess the characters.

GRAMMAR

GRAMMAR CHECK

Present Simple: Yes/No questions and short answers

We use auxiliary verbs and be (main verb) in Yes/No questions.

Do you like the Happy Prince?

Are all the people happy?

In the short answer we reuse the auxiliary verb or be (main verb).

Yes, I do.

No, they aren't (are not).

1 **Write answers for the questions about the Happy Prince's life at the start of the story. Use the short answers in the box.**

Yes, it is.	Yes, he does.	No, he isn't.	Yes, he can.	No, he can't.
Yes, he has.	No, he doesn't.	~~Yes, he does.~~	No, he doesn't.	Yes, they are.

a Does he live far away? ....Yes, he does.......

b Is he sad? ....

c Does he think about other people? ....

d Can he sing? ....

e Has he got any friends? ....

f Can he see the other people in his country? ....

g Does he like his palace? ....

h Does he ask questions about his people? ....

i Is his palace beautiful? ....

j Are his friends happy? ....

GRAMMAR CHECK

Information questions and question words

We use question words in information questions.

Where is the statue of the Happy Prince?

Why do the swallows fly to Egypt?

How many poor people are there in the city?

We answer these questions by giving some information.

On a column in the city.

Because it is warmer there.

I don't know. A lot.

2 **Complete the information questions with the question words in the box.**

Why	How many	What	How much
When	Where	Which	Who

a Q: .... Why .... does the prince cry?

A: Because his people are poor and unhappy.

b Q .... is the prince's ruby?

A: In his sword.

c Q: .... people does the swallow help?

A: A lot.

d Q: .... does the swallow give to the little girl?

A: A sapphire.

e Q: .... country does the swallow want to see?

A: Egypt.

f Q .... wants a new statue in the city?

A: The Mayor.

g Q: .... money have the prince's friends got?

A: A lot.

h Q: .... do swallows usually go to Egypt?

A: In the winter.

GRAMMAR CHECK

Verb + infinitive or –ing form

After the verbs *begin, forget, learn, like, need, remember, want,* and *would like* we use the infinitive with *to*.

'I need to go to Egypt,' says the swallow.

After the verbs *begin, finish, go, like, love,* and *stop* we use verb + –ing.

The poor young man loves dreaming.

3 **Complete these sentences about the story with the *to* + infinitive or verb + –*ing* form of the verb in brackets.**

a Everyone in the palace wants ....*to sing*.... (sing).

b The little boy begins .... (cry) for something new to play with.

c The people in the city love .... (look) at the gold statue.

d The statue can't go .... (dance).

e The swallow doesn't want .... (stay) in the city.

f The dressmaker's hands don't stop .... (move).

g The reed likes .... (move) her head from left to right.

h The poor young man needs ....
(buy) food and clothes.

i At first, the prince doesn't remember
.... (be) good to his people.

j The swallow would like ....
(fly) to Egypt.

k The gold statue never forgets
.... (help) the poor people.

l The swallow likes .... (talk)
to the prince.

GRAMMAR CHECK

Prepositions of movement

Prepositions of movement tell us how something moves.

up	↗	down	↘	into	→
out of	→	over	⌐⌐→	through	/\/\→
across	↗	past	→•	to	→●

4 Complete the text about the Happy Prince and the swallow with the prepositions in the box.

across	down	into	out of	~~past~~
over	past	through	to	up

The gold statue stands on a tall column in the city. The people walk a) ......*past*...... and look at the young prince. In the country, a little swallow flies b) .... the river and talks to his love, the reed. She doesn't answer him and so the swallow flies c) .... the city. From the sky, he looks d) .... at the buildings and the gold statue. He sits between the statue's feet and some water falls on him. He looks e) .... at the Happy Prince: he's crying. The swallow wants to go to Egypt but he stays and helps the prince. He takes the ruby f) .... the prince's sword. He flies g) .... the city and takes the ruby to a   poor dressmaker. He goes h) .... the house of a poor young man and gives him a sapphire.

He looks i) .... the windows of poor houses and sees the people there.

Now, when the people go j) .... the statue, they look happier.

GRAMMAR CHECK

Present Simple: third person –s

We add –s to the infinitive without *to* to make the third person (*he/she/it*) form of the Present Simple.

The prince lives in a beautiful palace.

The swallow tells the prince about the hungry children.

When verbs end in –o, –ch, –ss, or –sh, we add –es to make the third person form.

kiss – The swallow kisses the prince on the mouth.

When verbs end in consonant + –y, we change the y to i and add –es.

cry – The prince cries and his tears fall on the swallow.

The verbs *be* and *have* are irregular.

The prince has (got) a lot of money but he isn't (is not) happy.

We can use the Present Simple tense to re-tell a story.

5 Complete the text about the dressmaker with the verbs in brackets in the Present Simple.

The dressmaker a) ..is.. (be) always tired because she b) .... (work) a lot. Her little boy c) .... (lie) in bed with a fever. He d)............. (cry) and asks for something cold to drink. His mother e)........................ (have) no good food or water to give to him. The prince f) .... (watch) the woman and feels sad.

The swallow takes the ruby from the prince's sword and he g)............... (fly) across the city with it. In the palace, a young woman h) .... (wait) for her new dress. She i) .... (have) a lot of old dresses but she j)..................... (want) to wear her new dress. The swallow k)..................... (put) the ruby on the dressmaker's table and then he l) .... (go) away. He m) ....

(feel) much better now. That night, the prince n) .... (teach) the swallow something very important.

GRAMMAR CHECK

Comparative and superlative adjectives

	Comparative	Superlative
Short adjectives, such as *tall*	add –er *taller*	add the + –est *the tallest*
Adjectives that end in consonant + –y, such as *happy*	change y to i and add –er *happier*	change y to i and add the + –est *the happiest*
Adjectives that finish in a short vowel + consonant, such as *sad*	double the last consonant and add –er *sadder*	double the last consonant and add the + –est *the saddest*
Longer adjectives, such as *beautiful*	add more *more beautiful*	add the most *the most beautiful*

We use than after comparative adjectives.

The prince is bigger than the swallow.

Some adjectives are irregular.

good – better – the best   bad – worse – the worst   far – farther – the farthest

6 Write comparative sentences about the swallow and the reed.

a swallow / nice / reed ..The swallow is nicer than the reed..

b reed / beautiful / swallow ....

c reed / big / swallow ....

d reed / happy / swallow ....

e swallow / sad / reed ....

7 Write superlative sentences with these words.

a The prince / good / person in the city

   ..The prince is the best person in the city...

b The swallow / wonderful bird / the world

   ....

c The match girl / happy girl / her street

   ....

d The statue / expensive thing / the city

   ....

50

GRAMMAR CHECK

Linkers: and, but, so, and because

and links two parts of a sentence with the same idea.

The swallow loves the reed and he loves the prince, too.

but links two parts of a sentence with different ideas.

The swallow likes the sun, but he hates the cold.

so links two parts of a sentence talking about the result of something.

The people in the city are very poor <u>so the prince must do something</u>.

(result of first part of sentence)

because links two parts of a sentence talking about the reason for something.

The prince must lose his eyes <u>because he wants to help his people</u>.

(reason for first part of sentence)

3 **Complete the sentences with *and, but, so,* or *because*.**

a The Happy Prince lives in a palace .....*and*..... he is happy with all his friends.

b The prince can't help the poor people .... he can't leave his column.

c The swallow feels the prince's tears on his head .... he looks up.

d The swallow is kind, ... he doesn't want to stay in the cold city.

e The swallow takes the ruby to the dressmaker .... she can help her son.

f The poor young man can't think or write any more .... he is cold and hungry.

g The swallow wants to fly to Egypt, ... he stays with the prince.

h The bird is dying from the cold .... he knows it.

i The statue is ugly now .... it is grey.

⫽ DOMINOES Your Choice ⫽

Read *Dominoes* for pleasure, or to develop language skills. It's your choice.

Each *Domino* reader includes:
- a good story to enjoy
- integrated activities to develop reading skills and increase vocabulary
- task-based projects – perfect for CEFR portfolios
- contextualized grammar activities

Each *Domino* pack contains a reader, and an excitingly dramatized audio recording of the story

If you liked this *Domino*, read these:

The Tempest
William Shakespeare

Prospero, the Duke of Milan, and his daughter Miranda are far away from home, alone on an island in the middle of the Mediterranean Sea. They want to return to Milan . . .

Then, one day Prospero sees a ship near the island carrying his greatest enemies. Prospero, with the help of his magic and the island spirit, Ariel, makes a magic storm – a tempest – to bring them to the island.

Kidnap!
John Escott

One cold winter morning, a famous movie star and her teenage daughter are driving along a country road . . .

A blue van is waiting for them. Tom is in the van, but he's not a kidnapper – he's an artist. He usually draws pictures for adventure stories. Now he's in a real life adventure.

	CEFR	Cambridge Exams	IELTS	TOEFL iBT	TOEIC
Level 3	B1	PET	4.0	57-86	550
Level 2	A2–B1	KET-PET	3.0-4.0	–	390
Level 1	A1–A2	YLE Flyers/KET	3.0	–	225
Starter & Quick Starter	A1	YLE Movers	1.0–2.0	–	–

You can find details and a full list of books and teachers' resources on our website:
www.oup.com/elt/gradedreaders